TIME TO MEET
THE
ANGELS

MARK MIRAVALLE

Imprimatur for Part II:
Bishop Leo O'Reilly, Diocese of Kilmore, September 2014

Volume Nine Angels reprinted with permission. Copyright © Direction for Our Times, www.directionforourtimes.org

Published by:
Gabriel Press USA
313 High St.
Hopedale, Ohio 43976

For orders, please call: 740-937-2277
email:mary@motherofallpeoples.com
Or visit motherofallpeoples.com

ISBN: 978-0-9835597-2-6

Printed in the United States of America

Contents

Introduction

Amazing! The idea that there are invisible beings with most every perfection possible, who are always around us, who massively outnumber us, and who definitely out-think us! I'm not talking about aliens, nor about some fun fiction fantasy, whether it be Narnia or Middle Earth. I'm talking about the Angels.

But is this idea true? Yes, it is definitely true. How do we know? Because God said so.

There are about three hundred references to the exis- tence and the activity of these spiritual beings in the Bible, and God simply doesn't lie. He created these extraordinary creatures. Now it's up to us to appreciate them.

As a Professor of Theology at the Franciscan University of Steubenville for over a quarter century, I've seen a remarkable interest in "Angelology" or the Theology of the Angels over the last few years. In fact a few years ago, I began to offer a course on Angelology, and to my great surprise, the course has consistently filled up to capacity within the first few hours of class registration. It was also with great surprise that I found out that you could basically count on one hand the number of Catholic universities which offered any course on the Theology of the Angels.

Why then, a theology course on Angels, a very brief primer of which is offered here, in this little work? Because along with the new excitement about the Angels comes an unfortunate number of mistaken ideas about the Angels.

As much as I love the Christmas movie classic, "It's A Wonderful Life" (my personal favorite), it is at the same time packed with angelological errors! For example, Angels do not start as humans and then become transformed into angels based on their good deeds after death. Angels do not earn "wings" and they don't have physical bodies to begin with. Apart from the fun of cinema, these and many other mistaken ideas of the Angels have made their way into many a popular concept on Angels. Angels don't reproduce, they don't reincarnate, and they don't recycle. Nor are Angels part of God, nor part of us.

How do we know what's true about the Angels and what is false? Back to God. He is the Creator of the Angels and He is the only true Revealer about the Angels.

It is, indeed, time to meet the Angels.

The time is now to know, to appreciate, to befriend, and to love these heavenly beings who already know and love us, and who spend much of their efforts in guiding us to Heaven and protecting us from Hell.

We need to meet them, first of all, because *they are real*. We also need to meet them because we *need their powerful intercession* in the midst of the spiritual battle between good and evil which is being fought in dramatic and perhaps unprecedented fashion in our homes, at our schools, in our workplaces, in our neighborhoods, and throughout the world. As a father of eight great kids, and grandfather to three more great kids, I have to throw in my personal witness to having experienced the protective power of the Angels within my humble family time and time again. I know, with a personal moral certainty, that the Guardian Angels of my family have been extremely busy (oftentimes putting in big overtime hours) in protecting my brood at sports events, car rides, snowy evenings, and life decisions.

There is much we know about the nature and mission of Angels as contained in the Bible and in the Tradition of Christianity, which reveals this beautiful civilization of spiritual persons, far more numerous and far more intelligent than we are. God guides and protects the truth revealed in and through Jesus Christ as it develops through history in a living community of believers called the Catholic Church. I believe God has protected His truth about the Angels as found in the Bible to His living, breathing Church, to which He has granted an inspired authority, a successor to Peter that we call "pope," precisely to protect us from ourselves – our tendency to exaggerate or to edit His inerrant revelation.

Now some may retort, using a more "modern" secular mode of thinking, "I demand proof. I demand scientific and mathematical certainty that these so called "Angels" that I can't see or touch really do exist, or I simply won't accept them." To this, I would respond that you can't provide scientific or mathematical proof that your mother loves you, but I bet she does. In fact, you can't provide scientific or mathematical proof that you love anyone either, but I bet you do. In this beautifully complex and mysterious world we live in, we will find many things that, in themselves, do not lend themselves to scientific and mathematical certainty, they not only exist, they, in the last analysis, matter more than matter matters. Spiritual truths like love, beauty, truth, justice, and God Himself, are actually more real than things you can see and touch. And I believe the Angels fall into the same real and wonderful category.

Now, there are truths about the Angels that the Church states unequivocally – their existence, their nature and their mission. Other topics such as 'How do the angels know? How do they move? and How do they choose?' etc., are based on theological and philosophical deductions based on the biblical and traditional revelation of the Angels, topics which have engaged some of the greatest human minds and hearts in history.

St. Bonaventure, way back into the 13th century, wondered how clergymen could consider themselves educated Christians, but at the same time not be able to list, let alone discuss, the nine choirs of angels. We educated Christians of the 21th century may have some homework to do ourselves regarding the Angels!

Now, don't be put off by the footnotes and references in this little work. They are provided simply to give you the optimum information regarding what is being said here about these celestial beings. There are so many theories "floating around" about the Angels that I want you to know exactly where what I say about them here is taken from and by whom. This way, you can discern what sounds right and consistent with what Scripture and the Church reveals about our heavenly friends from the great body of Christian commentators.

Along with the sublime majesty of the angels revealed in Scripture and Christian Tradition, God, in His great generosity; has also provided yet another glance into the beauty, mission, and crucial importance of the Angels for us today.

In 2000, "Anne," an American mother of six who lives in Ireland, began to receive "locutions" or interior messages from Jesus, Mary, and other heavenly persons, which comprise a profound and inspiring message of mercy, conversion, hope and joy for today's world. This body of messages received through Anne is spread globally by the organization "Directions For Our Times" (see www. directionforourtimes.com). All of Anne's messages and writings have received the official Church "Imprimatur" by Bishop Leo O'Reilly of the Diocese of Kilmore, Ireland where Anne resides. Bishop O'Reilly, as the local bishop who has the task of first discernment regarding the supernatural character of these locutions, has also repeatedly granted permission for the international distribution of Anne's messages. These messages continue to lead to the remarkable spiritual fruits of conversion, healing and return to Jesus and the Church the world over. Everything regarding Direction For Our Times has been conducted in complete obedience to the rightful Church authority, and the results of a diocesan commission has been submitted to the Vatican's Congregation for the Doctrine of Faith for final evaluation.

Within the series of volumes dedicated to different themes contained within these messages, *Volume Nine* entitled, *Angels* contains eighteen messages from Jesus and Mary which discuss the extraordinary dignity, power, and role of Angels *for each one of us – and for the contemporary world as a whole.*

While it is, of course, your own personal prerogative whether to accept or reject these messages, (as the Church permits while she carries forth her own official examination,) I must honestly tell you that I personally believe these messages to be true, and powerfully so. You will find these messages confirm profoundly and completely the Church's official teachings regarding the Angels, while at the same time providing a new dynamic illumination and life to what the Church already believes about these glorious celestial persons.

What follows, then, in this little work, is this: first, a little summary of the nature and purpose of the Angels, as well as the classical "Nine Choirs of Angels" as derived from Scripture, Christian Tradition, and the most commonly accepted and respected of theological commentators. Secondly, the messages on the Angels from Jesus and Mary as received by Anne from August 23, 2004 to September 11, 2004, with each followed by a few specific "Points to Ponder" taken from the messages.

It is my prayer that this small glimpse into the cosmic profundity and celestial beauty of our angelic co-horts leads you to a deeper appreciation and, hopefully, love of these spiritual beings who already so very much love you, and will do all in their power to bring you home to heaven – to meet them, and the Triune God whom they serve, face to face.

Dr. Mark Miravalle
Professor of Theology and Mariology
Franciscan University of Steubenville

Part I

Time To Meet The Angels

Who and What are the Angels?

When we read passages like this from 8th century author and Church doctor, St. John Damascene, we get a first inkling of how resplendent, how mysterious, how beautiful are these remarkable spiritual beings we call "Angels":

The angels are secondary spiritual lights, who receive their brightness from the first Light, which is without beginning. They have no need of tongue and hearing; rather, they communicate their individual thoughts and designs to one another without having recourse to the spoken word.

Now, all the angels were created by the Word and perfected by the sanctification of the Holy Spirit, and in accordance with their dignity and rank, they enjoy brightness and grace ...

... When they are in heaven they are not on earth, and when they are sent to earth by God they do not remain in heaven. However, they are not confined by walls or doors or bars or seals, because they are unbounded ...

... The angels do not receive their sanctification by the Spirit as something due their essence. It is by the grace of God that they prophesy. They have no need of marriage, precisely because they are not mortal.

Since they are intellects, they are in places intellectually and are not corporeally circumscribed. For by nature, they do not have bodily shape and they are not extended in three dimensions ...

Whether the angels are equal in essence or whether they differ from one another, we do not know. Only God knows, who made them and knows all things. They do however differ from one another in brightness and station, either having their station in accordance with their brightness or enjoying their brightness in accordance with their station. They illuminate one another by the excellence of their rank or nature. Moreover, it is evident that the more excellent communicate their brightness and their knowledge to them that are inferior.

They are vigorous and prompt in the execution of the divine will and by a natural quickness they appear immediately in whatever place the divine pleasure may command. They watch over the parts of the earth and are set over nations and places in accordance with their disposition to the Creator. *They direct our affairs and help us.* Moreover, they are ever round about God for the very reason that in accordance with the divine will and command, *they are above us.*[1]

Who and what, then, are the Angels? Angels are created spiritual persons without bodies. They are pure spirits, created by God out of nothing as part of the wonder of divine creation. In the natural order, they are beings created with the closest possible image and likeness to God himself.

What is their principal goal? *To glorify God and to act as messengers of God to us.*

The *Catechism of the Catholic Church* confirms for us that "the existence of the spiritual, non-corporeal beings that Sacred Scripture usually calls "angels" is a truth of faith. The witness of Scripture is as clear as the unanimity of Tradition."[2]

Angels, then, are by nature *spiritual,* and by office *messengers.* St. Augustine, the great fifth century Father of the Church, makes this distinction in his famous quote about them: "Angel' is the name of their office, not of their nature. If you seek the name of their nature, it is 'spirit;' from what they do, 'angel."[3]

Both the Bible and Christian Tradition inform us that the Angels were created by God at the beginning of time. The Bible states repeatedly that all things were created by God, which include the creation of the Angels. As St. Paul reiterates: "In him (Jesus), all things were created in heaven and on earth, visible and invisible, whether thrones, or dominations, or principalities, or powers: all things were created by him and in him" (Col 1:16). The Fourth Lateran Council (an "ecumenical" or universal council of the Catholic Church) states back in 1215 that God "by his almighty power created together in the beginning of time both creatures, the spiritual and corporeal, namely the angelic and the earthly, and afterwards the human ...[4]"

It would be a mistake to believe that angels have existed from all eternity without a beginning. Another mistake is to believe that angels are extended parts of God (a position condemned at the First Vatican Council[5] in the 19th century). Or still more mistaken is the idea that angels are produced from other angels, for example, that a husband angel and wife angel unite to beget a "baby" angel. Angels are pure created spirits and because of this, they cannot reproduce, divide, spilt, or multiply – they can only be created.

Angels, as all persons, whether uncreated (God) or created (angels and us) have a thinking ability, an "intellect" and a choosing ability, a "will." *The Catholic Catechism* tells us: "As purely spiritual creatures, Angels have intelligence and will: they are personal and immortal creatures, surpassing in perfection all visible creatures, as the splendor of their glory bears witness."[6]

Three of history's greatest commentators on the Angels are Dionysius or "Pseudo-Dionysius", author of the early Christian work, *Celestial Hierarchy;* St. Thomas Aquinas, also known as the "Angelic Doctor" because of his masterful treatment on the Angels as found in his famous

13th century theological tome, the *Summa Theologiae;* and St. Bonaventure, the 13th century Franciscan Doctor of the Church referred to as the "Seraphic Doctor," whose angelic theology and spirituality pervades much of his renowned preaching and writings. Again, not all of the theories of the great angelological commentators such as these are considered official Catholic teaching. Still, they represent the most respected theological and philosophical reflections concerning the nature, mission, and purpose of the celestial choirs.

Let's now look at some of the most commonly asked questions about our celestial friends.

How do the Angels know things?

St. Thomas Aquinas tells us[7] that Angels do not know things as we humans do. Our human process of knowing starts with information of external things that comes to us through our external senses like sight, touch, hearing, etc. Then, through a process called "abstraction," we arrive at a core concept of the external thing. We call this an "idea."

Angels, on the other hand, sidestep this whole process. Angels have no external senses since they have no bodies. Instead, Angels are created with a God-given infused knowledge of natural things, like a computer that comes with a hard drive with all necessary information already downloaded. They have no need to get knowledge through any process, nor have they need to "ponder" over things, because their perfect intellects know the object in question immediately at the first moment the object is presented to their intellects. The angelic mind doesn't have to wait for any body process of a brain – they just know it.

But someone could ask, "If the Angels have a perfect infused knowledge of natural things, how then could they make mistakes? For example, how could some Angels make the tragic mistake of choosing against God, along with Lucifer during their experience of a "moral testing" and resulting fall from Heaven?" (cf. Rev. 12:7ff)

While the Angels were in fact given an infused knowledge of natural things, for example, the workings of nature, the universe, the cosmos, etc., they also were later given the revelation of *supernatural* things, such (as we'll discuss shortly) the future Incarnation of the Word to become flesh. Regarding this later supernatural revelation, the Angels could choose with their wills whether they would accept and obey this newly revealed supernatural truth of God becoming man, or not. Tragically out of pride, some angels chose not to accept the revelation of the Incarnation by God the Father. But this was *not* an error of their perfectly informed intellects regarding natural things, but a free will rejection of supernatural truth. In this way some Angels could, and did, make mistakes.

How do the Angels move?

As spiritual beings who have no bodies, Angels cannot move by physically going from one place to another. Actually, angels "move" by *exercising their power and influence in one place rather than in another place.* Wherever an Angel is exerting his power is where, we could say, that Angel "is."

Aquinas, the Angelic Doctor, also says that an Angel is not really contained in a place, but actually "contains the place."[8] Think of this example. When you let daylight into a room by pulling up the window shade, you can't capture the daylight by then pulling down the shade and trapping the daylight in the room. In the same way, the Angel is not contained by the space where he is exerting his influence, but is more "containing" that particular location, and cannot be trapped there by any physical or material barrier. Such is the awesome manner and mystery of the movements of a spiritual person with no bodily limit!

What about times when Angels appear to have bodies, like St. Raphael appearing as Azarias in the Book of Tobit?

An Angel can take on a temporary physical dimension for the sake of accomplishing a mission for God, or in protection of a human "ward." But this temporary body is not part of the essential or permanent nature of the Angel, and this temporary material aspect is just that – temporary. No Angel will have a permanent or resurrected body in Heaven for all eternity, as we will.

How do Angels communicate with each other?

Since Angels have no bodies, no external senses, or organs such as ears, they cannot hear or speak as we do. Angels do communicate though, but in a higher, "nonphysical" way. Angels communicate knowledge to one another in a non-material or *spiritual* way, and in this way they "speak" to each other. But it is a speech without sounds or uttered words. *Angels speak by the direct communication of knowledge from spirit to spirit.*[9] This exchange of ideas which we can call "angelic speech" is far more efficient than our human dialogue with its challenges of articulation or coming up with the right words. Angels exchange complete concepts with each other, leaving nothing vague or unclear.

St. Thomas Aquinas also taught that each Angel is a "species unto itself,"[10] meaning that each Angel, is as different from other Angels, as plants are different from animals, and animals are different from humans. Aquinas believed that since Angels have no material element or "bodiliness," that they could not be distinguished among members of their own species (unlike us humans, who are certainly distinguishable from other humans by our different physical bodies). If the Angelic Doctor is right, this speaks loudly to the magnificent uniqueness of each Angel. It would also reflect the profound individuality of each one of us: that our Creator would find us worthy to merit from Him the gift of such a unique creature to guide and guard each one of us through the challenges of this earthly life in pursuit of the heavenly home for which we were each created. This is heavenly affirmation par excellence!

What was the "Moral Testing" of the Angels?

It is the common consensus of the great Christian angelological commentators that after the Angels were created, but before they were given the glory of the beatific vision (seeing God "face to face" in heavenly grace for all eternity), they were to experience a *testing of the will.*

The nature of this moral test was the revelation by God the Father of the future Incarnation: that at some later time in history, God the Son would take on a human nature, and become man. When this would take place, the Angels would then be called upon to worship the Word made flesh, this "God-man" as their God and the King of the Universe.

The majority of angelic beings immediately pledged their obedience of mind and will to the manifest mind of the Father, and thereby received the beatific vision and eternal life of joy and peace in Heaven.

But one high Angel known as *Lucifer* (meaning "light bearer") rebelled in disobedience at hearing this divine plan, balked in pride at the idea that as an Angel who was created on a higher level of perfection than man, he would in turn have to offer worship to a "God-man" who would have an inferior human nature.

Some commentators from the Franciscan tradition (the Order of St. Francis) also maintain that when it was further revealed that the Word would receive His flesh through a woman, and that woman would from that time onwards be venerated by the all Angels as the "Queen of the Angels," Lucifer cursed, and uttered the rebellious words soon to become his fatal motto, "Non serviam" or "I will not serve."[11]

At the point of Lucifer's rebellious utterance, yet another tradition holds.[12] An Angel from the much lower eighth choir of Archangels responded to Lucifer's angelic pride and disobedience with the exclamation, "Who is like God? "Who would dare put their personal opinion on an equal plain with the divine mind and plan of the Creator?" This lower Archangel was Michael, whose name in Hebrew means precisely, "who is like God."

In reward for this proclamation of faith and fidelity, God raised Michael from the eighth choir of Archangels, to the highest levels of angelic dignity and power, and what Michael lacked in his created excellence as an Angel, God provided in the order of grace. Michael became the prince and leader of the heavenly army or "host" of Angels. St. Michael the Archangel and his host of warrior Angels then proceeded to cast out Lucifer, the Ancient Dragon, and a "third of the stars" or likewise disobedient angels, out of Heaven (cf. Rev. 12:7 ff).

A "yes" to the moral testing of the Heavenly Father merited eternal life with God in heaven. A 'no' to the moral testing led to the tragic expulsion of the fallen angels, where Satan and his demons initiated that experience of eternal separation from God we call "Hell."

Does this at all sound familiar? Even though our "moral testing" lasts a lifetime, the results of "yes" or "no" to God's revelation remains the same for each one of us.

Let's make our answer, "yes."

The Nine Choirs of Angels

Now to the glorious choirs of Angels!

Mortimer Adler, a famous British philosopher, would go around the world giving lectures on various aspects of Angelology. While he would see various well-intended members of his audience either nodding in slumber or feverishly fighting to keep their eyes open during his more scholarly lectures on various erudite aspects of angelological philosophy, he said that all perked up in their seats with eyes wide open in excited anticipation as soon as he announced that he would now be discussing the *nine resplendent choirs of Angels.*

The nine choirs of our heavenly friends, as found within their three respective hierarchies, represent great truth, great mystery, and certainly that obligation to put our heads as far back as possible, to look up vertically as high as possible, to see with our mind's eye the highest levels of God's created masterpieces and their diverse and mysterious functions.

Our principal sources here, once again, based upon the biblical revelation of the choirs and some of their tasks, are the renowned Dionysius, or "Pseudo-Dionysius"[13], with later commentaries by Pope St. Gregory the Great[14], St. Thomas Aquinas[15], St. Bernard of Clairvaux[16], and St. Bonaventure[17].

Basically, there are three "hierarchies" of Angels with three "choirs" within each *hierarchy*. An angelic hierarchy, according to Dionysius, is a sacred order of Angels who share in divine knowledge and activity, and who, in turn, guide and convey knowledge to those Angels lower to their own sacred order.[18] We can see, incidentally, why it is appropriate that the pope and bishops in union with the pope are referred to as the Church's "Hierarchy," as it, too, is a sacred order established by Jesus to convey truth to its members, and through them to the entire People of God. An angelic *choir* is a vast number of angels that share some common aspect of nature and function with other Angels of the same choir.

We have, therefore, three angelic hierarchies with three angelic choirs within each hierarchy. Each hierarchy has been designed by God to have its own specific purpose.

The first and highest hierarchy has the task of contemplating God in his infinite goodness, and also to contemplate the proper end or goal of all things of God and his creation. This is the primary function of the top three choirs of Angels: the Seraphim, the Cherubim, and the Thrones.

The second or middle hierarchy of Angels has the Godgiven task to receive illumination, that is, divine truth, knowledge and wisdom, from the first hierarchy, and to govern the material world based on that knowledge. This is the primary task of the middle three choirs: the Dominions, Virtues, and Powers.

The third or lowest hierarchy of Angels has the function of receiving illumination from the second hierarchy on what is to be done and to carry it out, particularly as it affects us the realm of humans. This is the task of the last three angelic choirs: the Principalities, the Archangels, and the Angels.[19]

Let's now say a few words about each particular angelic choir.

The Seraphim

The name, "Seraphim" comes from the Hebrew word, "saraph" which means "burning." The Seraphim, as the highest choir of Angels, possess a burning love for God, and these Angels excel in their awe-inspiring love of God.

The Seraphim are referred to twice in the Bible, in both cases in the Old Testament Book of Isaiah, Chapter 6. They are described as having six wings in three pairs. With the first pair, they cover their face out of reverence for being in the presence of God, which also reflects their great humility. With the second pair, they cover their feet because they are in the divine presence, and to represent their modesty. The third pair symbolizes the Seraphim's ability to "fly" in fulfillment of their task as heavenly messengers.

The primary function of the Seraphim is to sing unceasingly to God in endless praise of His holiness.[20] The Seraphim offer unceasing hymns of praise and contemplation of God through their perennial refrain, "Holy, Holy, Holy is the Lord of Hosts, the whole earth is full of his glory" (cf. Is. 6:1-7). These highest of all Angels can also have the task of participating in the purification of humanity. This is seen in Isaiah 6 when one Seraph purged the lips of the prophet Isaiah with burning coal: "Behold, this has touched your lips; your guilt is taken away, and your sin forgiven" (Is. 6:7).

The traditionally accepted Chaplet of St. Michael the Archangel (see Appendix II) dates back to the 18th Century. Tradition holds that it was transmitted to the Carmelite nun, Sr. Antonia d'Astonac through an actual apparition of St. Michael. This Chaplet specifically invokes Angels from all nine choirs for our needs and for their virtues. The St. Michael Chaplet invokes the first choir of Seraphim to intercede for humanity in granting us the grace to "burn with the fire of perfect charity."

The Cherubim

As the Seraphim excel in the love of God, so the Cherubim, the second angelic choir, excel in the truth of God. These exalted Angels excel in their knowledge of God and His truth. Dionysius explains that "the name Cherubim denotes their power of knowing and beholding God, their receptivity to the most high gift of Light, their contemplation of beauty in its first manifestation. They are filled by participation in divine wisdom."[21] St. Thomas Aquinas adds that the Cherubim are the channels of great wisdom to lower angels, and knowers of the "secrets of

God." They are, as members of the first hierarchy, close to the throne of God and contemplate his truth, beauty, and majesty unceasingly.[22]

The Cherubim are the first Angels mentioned in the Bible. When Adam and Eve are expelled from the Garden of Eden after their original human sin (remember the first "original" sin was actually an angelic sin), God places a Cherub with a flaming sword to protect the Tree of Life (cf. Gen. 3:24).

I am reminded here of the great insight of the former Vatican Ambassador from the Philippines, the Honorable Howard Dee. The Third Secret of Fatima, which was released by Blessed John Paul II in 2000, refers to an "Angel with a flaming sword," and only the intercession of Mary puts out the ongoing flames going towards the earth from the Cherub's sword. Ambassador Dee suggested that perhaps this was due to the fact that humanity has never before so attacked the contemporary "Tree of Life" with so many forms of attack on human life, from abortion (over 42 million a year worldwide), euthanasia, and now even efforts to clone human persons than in our present day. This is like saying to God the Father "We do not need you to tell us when to end life, and we soon we will not need you to begin life." The spirit of " I will not serve" surrounds today's Culture of Death.

Two golden Cherubim are also found on the Ark of the Covenant (Ex. 25:18-22) and their proximity to the Mercy Seat and the Ark also symbolize the close presence of the

Cherubim to Jesus, who is the ultimate "Divine Mercy," and to Mary, who by bearing Jesus became the new and everlasting " Ark of the Covenant." The Cherubim are further associated with being the "living Chariots of God" as referred to in Ezekiel 10 and Ps. 18:10. Ezekiel 1 describes the Cherubim as having "4 wings" and "human-like faces" (cf. Ezek. 1:1-23).

Interestingly, St. Thomas Aquinas speculated that Lucifer was probably a Cherub rather than a Seraph, since the burning love of Seraphim is opposite to pride, whereas great knowledge of truth, which the Cherubim possess, can more easily lead to pride. Yes, knowledge without love can be a very dangerous thing.

The Chaplet of St. Michael invokes the choir of Cherubim to "grant us grace to leave the ways of wickedness, to run in the paths of Christian perfection."

The Thrones

The Thrones, (*thronoi* in Greek, *throni* in Latin) the third choir of the first hierarchy, are mentioned explicitly by St. Paul in Colossians 1:16: "For in him [Jesus], all things were created, in heaven and on earth, visible and invisible, whether Thrones, or Dominions, or Powers, or Principalities." Dionysius tells us that the name, *Throne* denotes that which is "exempt from and untainted by any base or earthly thing ... They have no part in what is low, but dwell in fullest power, immovable and perfectly established in the Most High."[23]

The Thrones contemplate God in his essence of love and truth, and represent the firm, simple, and permanent contemplation of and submission to God. St. Bonaventure sees the Thrones as witnessing to a "steadfastness" in God[24], and St. Bernard of Clairvaux finds in this choir the virtue of "great tranquility."[25] St. Thomas adds that the Thrones are raised up to be "close recipients of God" in their very being and persons.[26] As a chair in a home remains permanently in its place unless the owner moves the chair, so the Thrones remain before God as in perpetual praise, to the delight of both the Creator and these most holy beings.

It is also through the Thrones, as the lowest members of the first hierarchy, that the middle hierarchy receives illumination about the "end" or goal of all things. This then leaves the middle hierarchy with the task of governing the created world, based on that knowledge of what all things in our created world are intended to do.

According to St. Michael's Chaplet, the Thrones are called upon to intercede to the Lord to "infuse into our hearts a true and sincere spirit of humility."

The Dominions

The fourth choir (and first of the middle hierarchy) are the Dominions, or sometimes called "Dominations" (*Kyriotetes* in Greek; *Dominationes* in Latin). Their name signifies the "Lordship" or dominion these Angels exercise over the lower choirs and over inferior created things. Also mentioned by St. Paul in Colossians 1:16, the Dominions have the role of heavenly government over things below them, and as such they preside over the actions of the Virtues and Powers. Dionysius says of the Dominions: "They are true lords, perpetually aspiring to true lordship and the source of all lordship .... They do not turn towards vain shadows, but wholly give themselves to that true authority, forever one with the Godlike Source of Lordship."[27]

St. Bonaventure says that "the power to command pertains to the Dominions."[28] St. Thomas adds that the Dominions "appoint those things which are to be done" by the lower Angels in the order of governing, and also make known to lower choirs the commands which come from God.[29]

The Dominions, therefore, are powerful Angels who possess dominion over much of creation, yet use their authority in service of the Kingdom, and not in any type of dictatorial power plays. This type of misuse of angelic power would only be present among the fallen Angels and their demonic choirs below.

The Chaplet of St. Michael invokes the Dominions to intercede that "the Lord give us grace to govern our senses and subdue our unruly passions."

The Virtues

The fifth angelic choir, the Virtues, do all, according to Dionysius, "with a God-like energy," and this strength "pours forth in everything they do."[30] Their name, "Virtue" (Greek, *dynameis,* Latin, *virtutes*) means "energy," "potency," or "strength." The Virtues receive everything from God with all their strength and power, and in turn, strive towards union with God with that same dynamic strength and power.

St. Paul speaks of the choir of Virtues in Ephesians 1:21, and St. Peter refers to the Virtues as "good angels" in 1 Peter 3:22. According to the Angelic Doctor, the Virtues "move the heavens (cosmos), direct the natural process of material generation, movement, and decay through the regular motion of nature."[31] The Virtues, therefore, control the elements, the seasons, the stars, even the sun and moon – in short, all aspects of nature. They also give to lower choirs the power of carrying out what is to be done.[32]

The idea of the Virtues actually controlling the turning of the seasons or the rotation of the planets may sound farfetched to some, but keep in mind what we can call "God's more the merrier principle" with His Church. The more God gets his creatures involved in His divine actions, the more his creatures are made holy, and the more God is given glory. Whenever free creatures use their freedom to cooperate with God in the fulfillment of his divine plan, it is both pleasing to God and a grace for the creature.

Every parent knows it is more satisfying when the child cleans his or her room on their own, even though the parent certainly can do the cleaning by their own efforts. The same is true for God. He could put forth all the efforts necessary for the governing of creation on His own and by His own power, but it gives him *more glory* when his angels cooperate in the fulfillment of God's will. For this reason, St. Thomas nicknamed the Angels, "God's secondary causes" because God chooses to do all possible in his creation through the intercession of His Angels.

According to St. Bernard, the Virtues also have the task of performing miracles and miraculous signs.[33] This would make sense, since a miracle is an event beyond the ordinary course of nature which is explainable only though the direct intervention of God, and the Virtues are the Angels directly in charge of the ordinary course of nature.

St. Michael's Chaplet asks the Virtues to request the Lord to "preserve us from evil and suffer us not to fall into temptation."

The Powers

The sixth choir, the Powers (Greek, *Exousiai,* Latin, *potestates*) reflect an irresistible power (though not tyrannical) that leads to God.[34] Their name obviously denotes the power of God, and they have as their task, according to St. Thomas, the ordering of *how* what has been commanded by higher choirs of Angels must exist to be carried out by the lower choirs of Angels.

St. Paul mentions the "good Powers" in Ephesians 3:10, and the "bad Powers" in Ephesians 6:12. Since some Angels probably fell from each choir during the moral testing and rebellion of Lucifer, there is some form of "evil hierarchy" of fallen angels in Hell. Each fallen Angel would retain the powers appropriate to its originally created level or choir. It is always tragic when God's gifts are used against God himself.

St. Bernard states that the Powers oppose the evil forces in the world,[35] and St. Bonaventure adds that the Powers may actually execute the chastisements of God in the order of justice.[36]

The Powers are certainly "Warrior Angels" who protect us and the world in general from the forces of evil spirits. The Chaplet of St. Michael calls upon the Powers to ask the Lord to "protect our souls against the snares and temptations of the devil."

The Principalities

The seventh choir of Principalities begins the lower hierarchy, the sacred order of Angels who, according to Dionysius and Aquinas, has the most to do with the 'affairs of men in carrying out the tasks ordained by the middle hierarchy."[37] The name, "Principality" (Greek, *archai,* Latin, *principatus*) indicates their "God-like princeliness."[38] The Principalities are the "princes" or "generals" of this lower hierarchy, who have as their primary responsibility the task to help and to protect the human race.

St. Bernard and others held that the Principalities presided over the "princedoms" or nations of the world, and are responsible for the wise governing of the world. It was therefore to this choir (both St. Bernard and St. Thomas believe), that the rise and fall of nations and the political shifts in power were in part responsible.[39]

Some angelological commentators also think that St. Jude singled out the choir of Principalities as the choir from which the most Angels disobeyed God and fell from Heaven with Lucifer to begin the reality of Hell (cf. Jude 1:6).

The Principalities, as the "spiritual generals," have the greatest authority of this lowest hierarchy in carrying out God's plan during the spiritual warfare for souls that takes place on each and every day of our life on earth.

St. Michael's Chaplet calls on the Principalities to intercede to God that He "may fill our souls with a true spirit of obedience."

The Archangels

St. Michael

The Archangels as the eighth choir are leaders and messengers of great importance in the world of man. The name "Archangel" indicates a role of leadership among Angels. They are the spiritual "officers" of the lowest hierarchy, and hold a middle place between the commanding Principalities and the Angels of the ninth choir. The Archangels are therefore commanders of the ninth angelic choir regarding the carrying out of God's will in human events.

The word, "Archangel" is mentioned twice in the Bible,

once by St. Paul in 1 Thessalonians 4:16 and again by the Apostle Jude, to St. Michael in Jude 1:9. These Angels, the great commentators informs us, preside over a multitude of peoples and also deliver the most important messages to humanity.[40]

The designation of "Archangel" can technically refer either to a "leader Angel" or more specifically to an Angel from this eighth choir. Regardless of which, the three Angels recognized by the Church with proper names and bearing the title, "Archangel" are St. Michael, St, Gabriel, and St. Raphael.

St. Michael, (Hebrew, *Micha'el* – "Who is like God"), is mentioned in Daniel 10:13 as "Michael, one of the chief princes." Daniel also says of this Archangel: "At that time shall arise Michael, the great prince who has charge of your people" (Dan. 12:1). St. Michael is, again, specifically referred to as "Archangel" by St. Jude (Jude 1:9).

The Church ascribes to St. Michael the role of being "Prince of the Heavenly Host," the leader of the angelic army assigned by the Father to route out Lucifer and his rebellious cohorts from heaven (cf. Rev. 12:7 ff.).

St. Michael the Archangel continues to battle against the forces of Hell in the contemporary spiritual war between good and evil. He is the ultimate "Warrior Angel," and the following "Prayer to St. Michael the Archangel" was universally promulgated by Pope Leo XIII at the end of the nineteenth century for the protection of the Church from the contemporary attacks of the evil one:

St. Michael the Archangel, defend us in battle. Be our protection against the wickedness and snares of the devil. May God rebuke him, we humbly pray; and do thou, O Prince of the Heavenly Host, by the power of God, cast into Hell Satan, and all the evil spirits who prowl about the world seeking the ruin of souls.

As Prince of the Heavenly Army appointed by the Father, St. Michael can be seen as the special Archangel at the service of God the Father.

St. Gabriel

St. Gabriel, (from the Hebrew, *Gebber* – man, and *'El* – God, "Man of God" or "Strength of God") is the Archangel at special service to God the Son and the Incarnation. Most of St. Gabriel's manifestations recorded in Scripture relate to the Birth of Jesus.

This great messenger Archangel appears in the Old Testament where he is sent by God to enlighten Daniel as to the meaning of a vision: "Gabriel, make this man understand the vision" (Dan. 8:16). Gabriel also brings Daniel "wisdom and understanding" (Dan. 9:21), and prophecies to Daniel the time when the Messiah will come (cf. Dan. 9:21-27).

In the New Testament, Gabriel fulfills the ultimate task of angelic messenger in bringing to the Virgin of Nazareth God's most important invitation in history: "In the sixth month, the Angel Gabriel was sent from God to a city in Galilee named Nazareth, to a virgin betrothed to a man whose name was Joseph, of the house of David; and the virgin's name was Mary. 'Hail, full of grace, the Lord is with you" (Lk. 1:26-28).

Keep in mind that Gabriel most likely did not simply memorize this message from the Heavenly Father to Mary, his greatest daughter. Rather the "Hail Mary" is largely the personal formulation of Gabriel himself, which is then conveyed to the Immaculate Virgin, (which of course captures the idea of the invitation as given by the Father). That's why the Hail Mary has been traditionally called the "Angelic Salutation." Every time we pray the Rosary (which we should daily!), we should also think of St. Gabriel and the Angels.

It is also this Archangel of the Incarnation that comes to Zechariah to announce the conception of John the Baptist, who will in turn prepare the people of Israel for the coming of the Messiah (Lk. 1:19ff).

As the special Angel of the Son and "Strength of God," some commentators believe that St. Gabriel may also be the Angel that comes to Jesus during this agony in the Garden, to strengthen him so as to endure and complete the greatest act of human suffering of all time.[41]

St. Raphael

St. Raphael, the third known Archangel, is the special Archangel of healing and consolation. The name "Raphael," which comes from the Hebrew words, *Rapha*

– to heal, and 'El – God (meaning "God heals"), reveals his role as a "healer of God."

The entire Old Testament Book of Tobit reveals the angelic person and role of St. Raphael as a healer of both physical and spiritual afflictions. Raphael takes on a temporary human appearance as "Azarias" to assist Tobit and his son, Tobias. His intercession leads to the spiritual healing of Tobias' future wife, Sarah, from the demon Asmodeus (Tobit 6:10ff). The hidden Raphael also directs Tobit to the ingredients necessary for the physical healing of Tobit from blindness (Tobit 6:6-8; 11:7-8). After the fulfillment of his heavenly mission, Raphael reveals his true identity to both Tobit and Tobias: "I am Raphael, one of the seven holy Angels who present the prayers of the saints and enter into the presence of the glory of the Holy One" (Tobit 12:15).

As the "Archangel of healing," some commentators speculate that St. Raphael may also be the "angel of the Lord" referred to in the New Testament (see Jn. 5:2-4), who stirs up the waters at the healing pool of Bethzatha:[42] "An angel of the Lord went down in certain seasons into the pool, and stirred up the water; whoever stepped in first after the stirring of the water was healed from whatever disease that person had" (Jn. 5:4).

In virtue of his mission of healing and comfort, St. Raphael has special relationship of service to the Holy Spirit, who as the Third Person of the Trinity is particularly known as the Divine Healer and Consoler.

The Angels

The ninth and lowest choir of Angels have the needs of humanity as their direct task and focus. The Angelic Doctor lets us know that this choir simply puts into action the specific commands of the Principalities and the Archangels in directing the affairs of the human family.[43]

By their nature and their God-given duty, the ninth choir is closest to our human world and our human needs. These Angels deliver messages that may not call for the importance of an Archangel. St .Bonaventure notes that Angels of the ninth choir "guard, comfort, and support humanity."

This is also the choir from which most (but not all) of our Guardian Angels come from.[44]

Psalm 91 speaks of the direct angelic protection that God provides for us: "For he will give his angels charge of you to guard you in all your ways. On their hands they will bear you up, lest you dash your foot against a stone" (Ps 91:11-12). Although these prophetic words apply ultimately to Jesus as our future Messiah, they also testify to Abba Father's care for each one of us through our Angels.

The most often quoted New Testament passage supporting God's great gift of an individual Guardian Angel to each human being are found in the loving words of Jesus Himself: "See that you do not despise one of these little ones, for I tell you their angels always behold the face of my Father in heaven" (Mt. 18:10).

The *Catechism of the Catholic Church* likewise confirms the gracious assignment of individual guardian angels by God to "protect and shepherd" each person: "From infancy to death, human life is surrounded by their watchful care and intercession: 'Beside each believer stands an angel as protector and shepherd, leading him to life.' Already here on earth the Christian life shares by faith in the blessed company of angels and men united in God."[45]

Friendship with Our Guardian Angels

Some of us have the tendency to give far too much attention to the powers of darkness, and far too little appreciation to the powers of goodness. For a moment, let's take an honest look at the two sides.

First, the *good side*. The good side, quite simply, is the side of Jesus. Who's on this side? We have the infinitely powerful and infinitely loving Trinity, God the Father, God the Son made man, and God the Holy Spirit. We have Mary, the Mother of Jesus, who is the Co-redemptrix with and under Jesus and Mediatrix of all graces, the Spiritual Mother of all peoples, and our most powerful Advocate after Jesus Himself. We have St. Joseph, who is the universal "Patron" or spiritual father of the Church, for what St. Joseph is to

Jesus, the Head of the Mystical Body of Christ, St. Joseph is to each one of us, the members of the Mystical Body of Christ – a powerful protector and intercessor. We have all the Saints in heaven as our brothers and sisters of great intercession. We have the Souls in Purgatory, who, even though they can't pray for themselves, they can pray for us. We have our earthly family of the Church, who battle alongside us in our pursuit of Christian holiness and happiness. And we have our extremely powerful Angels, all nine choirs of angelic intercession, coupled with the special protection and guidance of our own special Guardian Angel.

What about the bad side? Well, they have Satan, fallen angels, and fallen humans.

O.K. then – Whose side do you want to be on? Whose side has infinitely more power, more love, and more happiness? You got it. The good side.

Sometimes we need to keep in mind the power and goodness of the good side, knowing peacefully and joyfully that if we cooperate with the good side, the victory is clearly ours.

But cooperation includes tapping into the spiritual weapons provided for the good side by the Good God – and that crucially includes beginning and growing in friendship with your Guardian Angel.

Here we reach the ultimate, two-fold goal of this little work: 1) *to acknowledge the existence and the beauty of the Angels in general,* and 2) *to acquire a deep personal friendship with your Guardian Angel in particular.*

Once again, your own Guardian Angel has been "waiting" from the beginning of creation to know you, to love you, and to guide you home to Heaven. Truly, your Guardian Angel knows you better than any other human being, and loves you more than any other human being. For your Angel has been given both an angelic sharing in God's knowledge of you, and an angelic participation in God's love for you.

How, then, should we respond to such a heavenly gift, to such a spiritual person?

The answer is *friendship.*

We must acquire a living, personal friendship with our Guardian Angel. How is this done? Like any other Christian friendship. We must daily communicate with our Godgiven Guardian Angel in a consistent, ongoing relationship of ever-increasing love, trust, and confidence.

The starting point is prayer. The traditional "Prayer to the Guardian Angel," though simple, actually contains all the essential elements of beginning an authentic and binding friendship with your Angel Guardian. Some might find this prayer to be just too "childish" for an educated adult in the 21st century to pray. If so, I would suggest perhaps writing your own prayer to your Angels to recite daily. If not, you can stay with this one which is not, in my opinion, "childish," but rather "child-like," which is a good thing. It certainly continues to be my daily prayer:

Angel of God, my Guardian Dear,

To whom God's love commits me here;

Ever this day be at my side;

To light, to guard, to rule, and guide.

Thus begins your relationship with your personal and loving friend of light, which can (and should) then expand into more frequent daily communication between you and your Angel throughout the day. For example, ask your Angel to enlighten your mind as to the best decisions throughout the course of the day. Ask your Angel to strengthen your will as to make the most appropriate choices. Ask your Angel to protect you against the many trials and difficulties the day may bring.

In short, the goal is to include your Angel into *all your daily activities,* whether sublime or mundane. Keep in mind your Angel's God-infused knowledge of you and love for you which he wants to use in order to best lead you down your own unique path to Christian holiness and happiness – if you let him.

Four Ways to Cooperate with our Angels

Here are four ways in which we can actively cooperate with our Guardian Angels, in building a strong and lasting relationship of intimate love with them:

1. Adoration – Our Angels can teach us great things on how best to adore God, since it is so much part of their angelic nature to worship God well.

2. Contemplation – Our Angels can direct our minds and hearts as to how best to meditate upon and contemplate the great mysteries of God, Heaven, and all of God's revelation to us.

3. Expiation – Here, we can work in union with our Angels, since they, having no bodies, cannot offer their physical sufferings in reparation to God and for the conversion of sinners (cf. Col. 1:24). They can however consistently enlighten and inspire us to do so for God's glory, for the good of others, and for our own personal sanctification.

4. Guidance in our State and Vocation in Life – Far better than we can on our own, our Guardian Angel can direct us to the best possible fulfillment of the needs of our particular calling and state in life, helping us to make the best choices and actions to perfect ourselves in Christian love.[46]

Success or Failure?

The Venerable Fulton Sheen often concluded his weeklong priest retreats by stating that if the priest would commit to making a daily Holy Hour before the Blessed Sacrament, then his retreat was a success. If, on the other hand, the priest simply remembered some interesting insights of the retreat, but did not commit to a daily Holy Hour, then the retreat was a failure.

I believe the same holds true for our experience here with the Angels.

If this little work makes you ready to make a personal commitment to pray daily to your Guardian Angel as the start of a perpetual friendship in Christ, or as a renewal of a friendship that hopefully will continue for all eternity, then, by God's grace, **we have been successful.**

What a grace it is for us to know, to love, and to spread the truth and beauty of these sublime heavenly beings during our short time on earth, before we get to meet them, God willing, face to face in heaven!

Mary, as the Mother of Jesus Christ, the King of the Universe, is by virtue of her motherhood and her coredemptive role with the Redeemer, *Queen over all in His kingdom.* Her Queenship also includes the glorious realm of the Angels.

May Mary, the Queen of Angels, over whom God has given a special jurisdiction and authority, intercede for a greater knowledge and love of all Angels and, in particular, of our own Guardian Angels. May She, in the name and at the service of Jesus Christ, the Returning King, grant each one of us a greater gratitude to the Heavenly Father for the extraordinary gift of the Angels, as they work tirelessly for our personal holiness, our families, our human societies, and for peace for the entire world.

References

1. St. John Damascene, *Writings, Fathers of the Church,* Vol. 37, 1958, pp. 206-207.
2. *Catechism of the Catholic Church,* n. 328.
3. St. Augustine, En. In Ps. 103, 1,15:PL, 37, 1348.
4. Fourth Lateran Council, 1215, Denzinger 428.
5. First Vatican Council, Denzinger, 1804.
6. Catechism of the Catholic Church, n. 330.
7. St. Thomas Aquinas, *Summa Theologiae,* I. Q. 54, a. 1.
8. St. Thomas Aquinas, ST. I. Q. 52. a. 1. 9. ST I. Q. 107. a.1,2.
10. ST I. Q. 50, a. 4.
11. Cf. Jeremiah 2:20.
12. Cf. Fr. Pascal Parente, (former Dean of Theology and Professor at Catholic University of America), *The Angels,* p.57.
13. Dionysius or Pseudo-Dionysius, *The Celestial Hierarchy,* English translation as found in *Pseudo-Dionysius: The Complete Works, Classics of Western Spirituality,* Paulist Press, pp. 145-191.
14. Pope St. Gregory the Great, *40 Homilies on the Gospel, Homily 34.*
15. St. Thomas Aquinas, ST I. Q 108, a. 4, 6.
16. St. Bernard of Clairvaux, Cf. *On Consideration,* 5.
17. St. Bonaventure, Cf. *Collations on the Six Days; Sermons,* Opera, IX, p.611 ff.
18. Dionysius, *Celestial Hierarchy,* Ch. III. 19. Cf. ST, I. Q. 108, a. 6.
20. *Celestial Hierarchy,* Ch. VII.
21. *Celestial Hierarchy,* Ch. VII. 22. ST, I Q108, a. 6.
23. *Celestial Hierarchy,* VII.
24. St. Bonaventure, *2 Sent.* D. 9).

25. St. Bernard, *In Consid.,* V, 4.8. 26. ST, I. Q. 108, a. 6.
27. *Celestial Hierarchy,* VII.
28. St. Bonaventure, *Breviloquium,* 2. 8). 29. ST. Q. 108, a. 6.
30. *Celestial Hierarchy,* VIII. 31. ST, Q. 108, a.6.
32. Ibid.
33. St. Bernard, *On Consid.* 5.4.8.
34. *Celestial Hierarchy,* VIII.
35. St. Bernard, On Consid. 5.4.8.
36. St. Bonaventure, *Sermons, Opera,* IX, p. 611. 37.ST, Q. 108, a. 6.
38. *Celestial Hierarchy,* VIII.
39. Cf. St. Bernard, *On Consid.* 8.4.5.; St. Thomas Aquinas, *Summa Contra Gentiles,* 3. 80.
40. Cf. St. Bonaventure, *Breviloquim,* 2.8.
41. Cf. Parente, *The Angels,* p. 92.
42. Cf. Parente, *The Angels,* p. 102. 43. ST I Q. 108, a.6.
44. St. Bonaventure, *Breviloquim,* 2.8).
45. CCC 336; St. Basil
46. Cf .Teachings of the *Opus Angelorum Sanctorum,* www.opusange-lorum.com.
47. For more information on the Opus Angelorum Sanctorum, visit www.opusangelorum.com.
48. The specific approval by the Vatican Congregation for the Doctrine of Faith was made for members of the Opus Angelorum.

Part II

The Messages of Jesus and
Mary on the Angels as Received
by "Anne" a Lay Apostle

Yes, you do have to be careful when speaking about private revelation. I have served on several official Church commissions of investigation of reported private revelation, both in the United States and abroad. I know how serious they can be, and I know how beneficial they can be.

The Catholic Church's position regarding reported private revelation is at the same time "cautious" and "open." The Church is cautious because she cannot risk her reputation and office as guardian of the public revelation found in Scripture and Tradition (see Vatican II, *Dei Verbum,* n. 9-10), over a falsely reported private revelation by an individual. At the same time, the Church is "open" because throughout history, God has blessed his people with further private revelations which have served to encourage people to better live what is already revealed in the Bible and Tradition, but with a new strength, a new vitality and a new faithfulness.

Authentic private revelation has also served the people of God in knowing which aspects of the Bible should be especially highlighted in any given time period of the Church. This is true, for example, in the case of the contemporary emphasis on the "Divine Mercy" of Jesus as highlighted by the Church approved messages of Jesus to Polish sister and now saint, St. Faustina Kowalska.

I personally find the messages received by Anne, a lay apostle to be extraordinarily inspiring, beautiful, and grace filled. They have no doctrinal errors in them, and provide a message of Christian obedience, joy, and unity which comply entirely with the letter and spirit of the teachings of the Second Vatican Council and *The Catechism of the Catholic Church*. The local bishop, Bishop Leo O'Reilly, has given positive permission for the international distribution of these messages on two occasions, the most recent in August of 2011; has complied entirely with the directives of the Vatican's Congregation for the Doctrine of Faith concerning these messages; and is in the process of completing his own local Church investigation regarding these locutions.

Volume Nine of the messages given to Anne is on the Angels. Jesus gives twelve messages and Mary, the Mother of Jesus, follows with six messages which were delivered in 2004 concerning these most loving heavenly creatures of light. As the Church expressly permits the individual Christian to personally discern reported messages before she makes her final and definitive judgment (to which all should comply in full obedience), I invite you to prayerfully read the following messages which bring to life and dynamism what the Church has always taught and will continue to teach about our beloved Angels.

I discovered each message to be so packed with insight that I found myself underlining point after point in an effort to remember the major gems from the messages themselves. To save you some ink, I have put at the end of each message a few "Points To Ponder," a few of these gems for your own further meditation and appreciation.

August 23, 2004

Jesus

My children, I want you to be aware of every weapon in this spiritual battle. Seek Me first, and understand that I am God, all powerful and the Creator of All. You are part of a heavenly family and must remember that you have the whole of that family to help you. You understand that Our mother, Mary, is powerful. She is your first line of defense against evil and deception. You should pray the rosary every day. You have the sacraments. Holy souls or souls working for Me, and this I hope is each one of you, should attend Mass as often as possible. You should seek reconciliation with Me in the Sacrament of Penance. Also, Adoration of your Jesus in the Blessed Sacrament will give you an unlimited flow of graces which will grant you peace and guidance. You have the saints in heaven. They wish to help you. Ask them each day for their intercession. Study their lives and you will understand why they are such effective helpers. They walked your walks already. You have Me, in the silence of your heart. Spend time there each day.

My children, another weapon you have at your disposal is angels. Angels are heavenly servants who do not experience humanity. They are pure goodness and heaven is filled with them. You will enjoy their company immensely when you come home to Me. These beautiful beings are active in your world now and have always been. In these days, given the necessity of great heavenly help and intervention, I have given the angels, along with the saints, permission to be even more apparent. They will surround you if you ask them. Ask Me for angels to assist and protect you and you shall have them. I will describe their attributes and you will understand that you are never alone because you are surrounded by angels. You see, My children, there is so much talk of the enemy and the enemy is so glorified in your world, that many souls forget that heaven is far and away more powerful than the pitiful band of bitter ones who serve darkness. These want only your misery. Conversely, the unlimited number of good and holy servants, want only your joy and safety. But your prayers are necessary to mobilize all of this power. In these times, many souls spend time with darkness through their activities and recreation. In doing so, souls are inviting the enemy's companionship. If souls do not invite our companionship, through prayers and requests, we do not force ourselves. So surround yourself with all that is Light and the enemy will avoid you. Ask for an honor guard of My angels and you will be enveloped in powerful beings from heaven who will insure that you complete your missions in safety. Children, you are God's little creatures. You will not be abandoned.

Points To Ponder:

- *I have given the angels, along with the saints, permission to be even more apparent. They will surround you if you ask them.*

- *Ask Me for angels to assist and protect you and you shall have them.*

- *... Many souls forget that heaven is far and away more powerful than pitiful bands of bitter ones who serve darkness.*

- *So surround yourself with all that is Light and the enemy will avoid you.*

- *Ask for an honor guard of My angels and you will be enveloped in powerful beings from heaven who will ensure that you complete your mission in safety.*

August 24, 2004

Jesus

The angels surround you, My dear ones. They minister to you in so many ways that I could not clearly explain this to you. I am going to give you some idea of these heavenly friends, however, so that you will understand the strength on your side. When you attend Mass you are praying and worshipping with thousands of angels. Your guardian angel goes with you, of course, and is so grateful for the opportunity to rest in the heavenly companionship of his fellow angels. These beings of light pay rapt attention and take such joy in praising Me. Truly, each church is filled with angels. When you enter a church and find it empty, that means that you can see no other human. But there are angels present and they welcome you as they welcome your angel guardian. This loyal servant of Mine, your special guardian, prays for you without interruption. When you are safely on the path to heaven, this angel then begins to petition heaven for greater and greater spiritual gifts. Your angel can communicate with the saints in heaven and often seeks out their intercession for you. When you are working with your angel and with the saints, you will find yourself making sublime spiritual progress because the gifts being secured are of the deepest and sometimes most indiscernible variety. You are often making progress that you do not feel, little soul, but your angel is watching it closely. When something threatens your spiritual progress, your angel attempts to warn you. He does this in many ways. You often hear whisperings, what many call your conscience. This is your angel attempting to persuade you that whatever you are considering will be bad for your cause. Your angel can anticipate danger so you should always ask him to be alert and assist you. When a soul tries to follow a path of goodness, that person's angel is so pleased. He joyfully sings praise to heaven for the goodness of the soul entrusted to his care. When a person strays off the path of goodness, the angel is saddened and heavyhearted. Regardless of the darkness practiced by a soul, his angel remains by his side, petitioning heaven for graces to convert his charge. When an angel guardian anticipates that the soul in his care is about to lose eternity in heaven, that angel stops at nothing to gain intervention. This beautiful being of love will obtain the intercession of many holy souls, asking for prayers and sacrifices. He will seek out the intercession of the saints, and he will stop at nothing to veer his charge away from damnation. It is only at the gates of hell itself that an angel guardian will relinquish hope. Speak to your angel, little souls. Believe in his presence. I, Jesus, want you to have every consolation available to you on your earthly journey. Take advantage of this good and constant friend.

Points To Ponder:

- *When you attend Mass you are praying and worshipping with thousands of angels. Your guardian angel goes with you, of course, and is so grateful for the opportunity to rest in the heavenly companionship of his fellow angels.*

- *... Each church is filled with angels.*

- *This loyal servant of Mine, your special guardian, prays for you without interruption.*

- *Your angel can communicate with the saints in heaven and often seeks out their intercession for you.*

- *When something threatens your spiritual progress, your angel attempts to warn you ... you often hear whisperings many call your conscience. This is your angel attempting to persuade you that whatever you are considering will be bad for your cause.*

- *Speak to your angel, little souls. Believe in his presence ... take advantage of this good and constant friend.*

August 25, 2004

Jesus

My children who seek the Light are surrounded by heavenly beings. These beings, My angels, seek My will. There is no darkness in them. They do not sin. They do not serve one day and abandon the Divine Will the next day. They know Me and worship Me. Because they have a great depth of heavenly knowledge, they can anticipate heaven's wishes and heaven's designs. They know exactly what I am seeking in each situation. They know exactly what will bring a soul closer to perfection in each moment. Therefore, their counsel and direction is perfect. They do not steer a soul away from Me. They could not. They seek only the Divine Will. As such, My dear children, they are the perfect companions for you. You must remember them and remember their presence. They have illumination that you do not have. So you may be uncertain on how to proceed in a given moment. You should ask your angels for counsel, understanding that the way they direct you will be My way and the best way for you, given every single circumstance in your life. Angels can read souls at a glance. They recognize unsuitable companions. Ask your angel to protect you from relationships that will pull you away from Me. There are times when this is very important and you should always be aware that your companions will influence you. Ask the angels to protect your children and to help your children find suitable companions. Every wise parent knows that children are influenced by their companions and if a child's friends are not following a path that leads to Me, their own child will be diverted. This is a serious risk for children and adults. Keep holy company, My dear ones. The angels will help you.

Points To Ponder:

- *These beings, my angels, seek My will. There is no darkness in them. They do not sin.*

- *They know exactly what will bring a soul closer to perfection in each moment. Therefore their counsel and direction is perfect.*

- *My children, they are the perfect companions for you. You must remember them and remember their presence. They have illumination that you do not have.*

- *You should ask your angel for counsel, understanding that the way they direct you will be My way and the best way for you, given every single circumstance in your life.*

- *Ask your angel to protect you from relationships that will pull you away from Me.*

- *Ask your angels to protect your children and to help your children find suitable companions.*

August 26, 2004

Jesus

When a soul is experiencing difficulty, I send additional angels to assist. In this way, a soul has heavenly influences to help counteract the worldly influences with which he is struggling. If a soul requests heavenly help, I can send even more assistance in the way of angels and graces. "How does this help, Jesus," I hear My little ones asking. It helps because when you ask Me for help, and I send angels, you are surrounded by these beings who are praying for you and petitioning saints to pray for you. They influence the actions of others, also, and can obtain earthly assistance for you by inspiring a holy soul to come to your aid at just the right time. How many times have you said that this one or that one was a life saver to you? Do you think that this happened accidentally? Hardly, little ones. I sent that soul into your life to assist you and that soul was inspired by the promptings of the little servants of light who surround you. There is so much happening in your world that is necessarily invisible to you. If you saw all of these things you would not struggle at all and then there would be no need for your beautiful acts of faith and love and obedience to Me. These things provide heaven with delightful music from the earth. During this time, when the majority do not serve, I am particularly consoled and responsive to those who are trying their best to benefit the Kingdom. So be brave and confident. You are part of a team, as we continually remind you, and you shall have all of the help you need, and more help besides.

Points To Ponder:

- *When a soul is experiencing difficulty, I send additional angels to assist.*

- *If a soul requests heavenly help, I can send even more assistance in the way of angels and graces.*

- *It helps because when you ask Me for help, and I send angels, you are surrounded by these little beings are praying for you and petitioning saints to pray for you.*

- *I sent that soul into your life to assist you and that soul was inspired by the promptings of the little servants of light who surround you.*

- *So be brave and confident. You are part of a team ... and you shall have all the help you need, and more help besides.*

August 27, 2004

Jesus

Yes, it is true. The beings of the Light surround My little soldiers. And if you ask for more help, you will receive more help. There is no question of My remnant being abandoned. The only thing that hampers heavenly assistance is a lack of faith on the part of My children. When faith is weak, souls fear they are vulnerable. This fear can be exploited by those who would like to see souls turn away from Me and turn back to the world. You must be very determined to walk My path during this time of transition. I am relying on My children to salvage as many brothers and sisters as possible through their work with Me. Be confident in the ones who surround you, the angels. They are your assistants, so to speak. Treat them with the greatest of love and respect, often acknowledging their presence. You do this through little prayers, perhaps prayers thanking God for sending you such an honor guard. You do this when you are in a situation where you do not know what to do or what to say. You can then say, "Angels from heaven, direct my path." This prayer is short and yet you are asking for clear direction to the heavenly course. This is a powerful and pleasing prayer and I will give great graces to the answering of this prayer. Use this often throughout your day and you will not be disappointed in the help you will receive through it. Just as the saints have enhanced powers during this time, so do the angels. You will want to use everything at your disposal and you will truly become an invincible servant of God. I intend great holiness for all who answer My call.

Points To Ponder:

- *The only thing that hampers heavenly assistance is a lack of faith on the part of My children. When faith is weak souls fear they are vulnerable.*

- *You must be very determined to walk My path during this time of transition. I am relying on My children to salvage as many brothers and sisters as possible through their work with Me.*

- *Be confident in the ones who surround you ... treat them with the greatest of love and respect, often acknowledging their presence.*

- *You do this through little prayers, perhaps prayers thanking God for sending you such an honor guard.*

- *You do this when you are in a situation where you do not know what to do or what to say. You can then say: "Angels from heaven, direct my path" ... This is a powerful and pleasing prayer and I will give great graces to the answering of this prayer.*

August 28, 2004

Jesus

My children, you have advanced a great deal with regard to knowledge of your physical world and even in the study of the human body. But what you have discovered and uncovered is but a tip of the limitless body of knowledge that heavenly beings own. They understand how the physical body works and how it stops working. They understand the intimacies of each cell in the human body and with a glance can tell exactly what is wrong with someone who is sick. These angels, who work tirelessly for you and for your world, truly have constant access to the greatest store of knowledge and wisdom. These are good companions to have working alongside you. Your struggles are child's play to them in the sense that they have the answers to life's questions. They can advise you and counsel you but they cannot force you. So if you are determined to sin, they cannot stop you. At times, though, they can divert you from an occasion of sin. At other times they can secure a state of disinterest in sin when you are at risk. You will wonder at your disinterest in something that possibly had attracted you in the past. Thank the angels for this grace because they have obtained this state for you through their prayers. They rally support from your friends in heaven and know exactly who to attend for each type of assistance. When you understand how much your angel guardian has done for you in your lifetime, you will be overcome with gratitude, both to your tireless friend and to the God who assigned this little creation of love to you. Thank him and talk to him.

You are not like a silly person who imagines things in doing so, but like a very wise man who looks at the universe and understands that he does not understand its secrets. Sit in silence with Me, little ones, and I will give you this wisdom. Pray to the angels and they will obtain it for you.

Points To Ponder:

- *They understand the intimacies of each cell in the human body and with a glance can tell exactly what is wrong with someone who is sick.*

- *These angels, who work tirelessly for you and for your world, truly have constant access to the greatest store of knowledge and wisdom.*

- *Your struggles are child's play to them in the sense that they have the answers to life's problems. They can advise you and counsel you but they cannot force you.*

- *When you understand how much your angel guardian has done for you in your lifetime, you will be overcome with gratitude, both to your tireless friend and to the God Who assigned this little creation of love to you.*

August 30, 2004

Jesus

The universe is filled with angels. How could it not be? The universe belongs to Me and to all who follow Me. When you look up into the sky, there are angels. When you die and leave your body, you will see them. You will be comfortable with them and they will be comfortable with you because you are all part of My creation. You, My little souls who served in the world, are especially precious to Me, of course, and you will be rewarded accordingly. In your time of service, you will come across many a soul who is in need of conversion. Perhaps you are moving quickly in and out of someone's life, as on a train, or while traveling in another way. You sense, though, that a soul is in distress or unhappy or struggling with an addiction that prevents him from possessing his soul. Pray to his angel guardian. Say, simply, "Angel guardian, thank you for your constant vigil over this soul. Saints in heaven, please assist this dear angel." That is very simple and yet you have secured fresh hope and assistance to this little being of light. In this way, the soul's angel can take your prayer and secure additional graces. Children, have the greatest faith in prayer. Truly, your prayers are saving souls and changing the course of events in the world. Continue to petition heaven for the graces you need to help others. We are answering, dear souls. We are answering.

Points To Ponder:

- *The universe is filled with angels ... When you look up into the sky, there are angels.*

- *In your time of service, you will come across many a soul who is in need of conversion.*

- *Pray to his angel guardian. Say simply, "Angel guardian, thank you for your constant vigil over this soul. Saints in heaven, please assist this dear angel."*

- *In this way, the soul's angel can take your prayer and secure additional graces.*

- *Truly, your prayers are saving souls and changing the course of events in the world.*

August 31, 2004

Jesus

In order to live fully, you must consider your universe, both what is seen and what is unseen. Often it is the unseen that moves souls, and souls who allow for heavenly influences and guardians live more fully and more securely. My children, with all of the divine assistance surrounding you, you truly lack for nothing. I would not ask you to complete the missions I have entrusted to you and not give you adequate support. The support is there. You simply have to utilize it. If you are working on a project for Me and feel you have encountered an obstacle, joyfully ask the angels in heaven to remove it. Be peaceful as you know that I will not hold you accountable for things that you cannot change. Work steadily, aware that you are surrounded by My friends, in the form of angels, but also saints. With the heavenly company you are keeping, you will learn to be at peace in everything. You will learn to take the heavenly view of every situation and every person. For example, perhaps you are placed in the presence of a soul for whom you feel repugnance. A worldly approach would be to escape this person's presence as quickly as possible. Now, after considering the presence of the angels and saints, you might discuss the matter silently with them. They may inform you that this soul is in great pain, which he masks with an unpleasant or aggressive exterior. Perhaps his soul is in distress and longs for the heavenly union you enjoy. Perhaps he has been badly injured by those who were supposed to love him or maybe he is sick in body. Maybe, My friends, life has disappointed him and there was no Jesus to heal his wounds. Now, would you not consider that situation differently in light of these possibilities? Your angelic friends, including this man's angel guardian, might explain this to you and urge you to treat him with exactly what his soul needs to creak open the smallest bit and allow Me inside. You know what I am capable of, given room in a soul. It becomes a very different situation, does it not? While you are on earth, you may not see what your prayers and love accomplished for this soul. But you will see it in heaven. You will see all of the fruits of your little acts of self-denial and love when you arrive here. My friends, how differently you will live, given a constant awareness of your heavenly companionship.

Points To Ponder:

- *My children, with all of the divine assistance surrounding you, you truly lack for nothing ... The support is there. You simply have to utilize it.*

- *If you are working on a project for Me and you feel you have encountered an obstacle, joyfully ask the angels in heaven to remove it.*

- *With the heavenly company you are keeping, you will learn to be at peace in everything. You will learn to take the heavenly view of every situation and every person.*

- *Your angelic friends, including this man's angel guardian, might explain this to you and urge you to treat him with exactly what his soul needs to creak open the smallest bit and allow Me inside.*

- *My friends, how differently you will live, given a constant awareness of your heavenly companionship.*

September 1, 2004

Jesus

My dear ones walk through their lives in the company of angels. In some places there are more angels than in others. When a holy person feels an unexplained joy or an unexplained sense of peace, that person often has entered a place that is filled with angels for one reason or another. My dear servants may find that they are drawn to a place and cannot determine why this is so. Perhaps that place was the scene of a holy action or actions. Perhaps a house was home to a holy soul. Perhaps great sacrifice or love was present in a given place. These places draw angels, as well as people, and often angels will remain, or revisit. In the same way, if a soul is working against Me, that soul may find that he is terribly uncomfortable in certain places. He perhaps is uncomfortable because he does not like the company of angels, knowing instinctively that he is not an appropriate companion for heaven's little beings. If he has the remotest wish to repent, these places will bring thoughts of sadness to his mind and he will long for something indiscernible. This longing is indiscernible to the consciousness of this person, but it is simply a longing for goodness. Thoughts of a good person he has known will come into his mind and he will view his life in isolation from Me clearly. For some, this will cause a man to flee in anger. He has no wish for Me. For others, a visit to such a place will cause him to begin the process of change, of renewal, of repentance. Invite angels into your homes and workplaces. Ask heaven to surround you with them in every meeting and conversation. Send angels often to those in the state of sin so that their poor little hearts will long for the oxygen of forgiveness. These strategies I give you are all part of the great renewal. You are preparing souls and preparing the earth. You are My friends.

Points To Ponder:

- *When a holy person feels an unexplained joy or an unexplained sense of peace, that person often has entered a place that is filled with angels for one reason or another.*

- *Perhaps great sacrifice or love was present in a given place. These places draw angels, as well as people, and often angels will remain or revisit.*

- *In the same way, if a soul is working against Me, that soul may find that he or she is terribly uncomfortable in certain places.*

- *If they have the remotest wish to repent, these places will bring thoughts of sadness to their minds and they will long for something indiscernible.*

- *Invite angels into your homes and workplaces. Ask heaven to surround you with them in every meeting and conversation. Send angels often to those in the state of sin so that their poor little hearts will long for the oxygen of forgiveness.*

- *These strategies I give you are all part of the great renewal.*

September 2, 2004

Jesus

There are many ways in which a soul can serve the Kingdom. In these times, though, more than in the past, souls are called upon to evangelize for Me. This means I need souls to bring Me to others. We must seek out each lonely, hurting soul who is isolated from his divine family. If you bring Me to a soul, I can melt that soul's heart and fill it with joy. The soul can then begin to learn about the vast family of love that seeks to draw him back. Dearest little servants of the Savior, My angels will direct you to these souls. Be alert to their promptings and whispers because they see everything and they know who needs your assistance. If you feel an impulse to approach a soul with these words, do so. Trust those instincts. Even if a soul initially ridicules you, he will eventually face a time of fear or anguish, and, searching for some kind of comfort, he will reach for the book you have given him. If the words are not there, he cannot reach for them. If the Volume has been given to him, he will open it. Be at peace at the reactions of others. You cannot force a soul to learn about Me, but you can suggest that he do so. You can give witness to My presence by talking about your love for Me and the graces you have received from Me. Talk about peace. Talk about joy. Talk about calm. Do not talk about the enemy. There is too much emphasis placed on the minimal power of the one who seeks destruction. When a soul is truly following Me, there is little the enemy can do to divert that person. Fear nothing. Why would you fear when you have a universe filled with heavenly beings who await your requests and petitions? Listen carefully to them and My angels will direct you to the souls who require your help.

Points To Ponder:

- *In these times, though, more than in the past, souls are called upon to evangelize for Me ... I need souls to bring Me to others.*

- *My angels will direct you to these souls. Be alert to their promptings and whispers because they see everything and they know who needs your assistance. If you feel an impulse to approach a soul with these words, do so. Trust those instincts.*

- *If the Volume has been given to them, they will open it.*

- *You can give witness to My presence by talking about your love for Me and the graces you have received from Me.*

- *Talk about peace. Talk about joy. Talk about calm. Do not talk about the enemy.*

- *Fear nothing. Why would you fear when you have a universe filled with heavenly beings who await your requests and petitions?*

September 3, 2004

Jesus

My dear ones, you must learn to work as part of a team. Any task entrusted to you has also been entrusted to one or more angels, who are assigned to assist you. You see that you are never alone. Even the smallest task you must complete will have at least one angel attached. Your angel guardian is always with you. So you are wrong to feel overwhelmed by the mission given to you because you bear only one part of the responsibility. When you feel heavily burdened, you must ask yourself what I am requesting of you in this moment. Then you must pray to the angels to help you. Then you must pray to the saints to intercede for you. After that, you must remember that Mary, your heavenly mother, is near you, and also interceding for you. She watches closely for any sign that you are struggling. After all of that, remember that I, Jesus Christ, the God of All, am with you. Ask yourself again if you are overwhelmed. When you are worrying about the future there is always a risk of becoming frightened because you have the graces only for the present. You are given what you need for this moment. Remain with Me, with Mary your mother, and the saints and angels. We are not in the future. We are not in the past. We are here, in the present, and you are one part of our powerful team.

Points To Ponder:

- *You must learn to work as part of a team. Any task entrusted to you has also been entrusted to one or more angels, who are assigned to assist you.*

- *Even the smallest task you must complete will have at least one angel attached.*

- *When you feel heavily burdened, you must ask yourself what I am requesting of you in this moment. Then you must pray to the angels to help you. Then you must pray to the saints to intercede for you.*

- *Mary, your Heavenly Mother, is near you and also interceding for you. She watches closely for any sign that you are struggling.*

- *After all of that, remember that I, Jesus Christ, the God of All, am with you.*

- *Remain with Me, with Mary your Mother, and the saints and angels ... you are one part of our powerful team.*

September 4, 2004

Jesus

With eyes of faith you must look for My angels. They are with you, My dear struggling souls. You must believe that you are not alone because you will then live differently. When a soul has confidence that he is part of a heavenly team, he walks in quiet certainty that all will be well. This soul understands My power and My dominion over his universe. His sufferings are accepted and given to Me as part of the offering that is his life. Very little can disturb this soul because he understands that all on earth is temporary. Truly, as long as he follows My will, he is at peace. Dear children of this world, you must strive for this unity with the Divine Will in your life. Only with unity can you move peacefully through a world that is not peaceful. And that is My wish for you. Peace, both for your little soul, and for the souls of those who encounter you. You must accept My peace in your soul because only in that way will peace spread. Your example to others is an important part of My plan. So when I ask you to be at peace, I am really pleading with you. Living in My peace is part of what I am requesting of you. When tempted toward agitation and upset because of events around you, you must resist and maintain your heavenly bearing, mindful that I am God.

Points To Ponder:

- *With eyes of faith you must look for My angels. They are with you ...*

- *When a soul has confidence that she is part of a heavenly team, she walks in quiet certainty that all will be well. Very little can disturb this soul because she understands that all on earth is temporary. Truly, as long as she follows My will, she is at peace.*

- *Dear children of this world, you must strive for unity with the Divine Will in your life. Only with unity can you move through a world that is not peaceful.*

- *Your example to others is an important part of My plan. So when I ask you to be at peace, I am really pleading with you.*

- *When tempted toward agitation and upset because of the events around you, you must resist and maintain your heavenly peace, mindful that I am God.*

September 6, 2004

Blessed Mother

While I lived on earth, I was always aware that heaven existed. I knew that angels actively sought to console and assist us in our troubles. This awareness did not come from my physical senses, those of sight or hearing, but from my spiritual sense, of loving and being loved. You must begin to use your spiritual senses, the senses of your soul. These senses, which you can understand as the living Holy Spirit, will guide you. In everything I sought unity with my Creator. He, God, did not disappoint me. Because I constantly sought unity, I grew in the awareness that earth is not separated from heaven in terms of space. Heaven is present on earth in the form of the Spirit and the spiritual presence of the souls who have gone before us and, of course, God's beautiful angels. How I love these beings of light. They seek only His will and only goodness. Truly, they are the difference between darkness and salvation to many souls. They are always with me and they are always with you. Little children of my Immaculate Heart, thank God for His angels. Thank God for the beautiful inspirations that have come from His angels. Have you ever been helped by a stranger? You must thank your angel guardian for procuring that help. Look with faith at your world and you will see that angels are everywhere. In these times of great change, the angels will be very active in the lives of the faithful ones who courageously assist heaven. I am with you, my little ones. I am always with you.

Points To Ponder:

- *You must begin to use your spiritual senses, the senses of your soul. These senses, which you can understand as the living Holy Spirit, will guide you.*

- *Heaven is present on earth in the form of the Spirit and the spiritual presence of the souls who have gone before us, and, of course, God's beautiful angels.*

- *How I love these beings of light. They are always with me and they are always with you.*

- *Little children of My Immaculate Heart, thank God for His angels. Thank God for the beautiful inspirations that have come from His angels.*

- *Look with faith at your world and you will see that angels are everywhere.*

- *In these times of great change, the angels will be very active in the lives of the faithful ones who courageously assist heaven.*

September 7, 2004

Blessed Mother

I am joyful to be talking to my little ones about angels because I know that the thought of angels makes you happy. So often in these times we are discussing difficult matters, so it is a relief for me to talk to you about something that is lovely and good. Children, your Jesus has asked that you walk in peace. He needs this from you, as His plan cannot be realized unless you cooperate with that request. Only through each one of you will peace flow into your troubled world. So, because this is so important, I am going to make a suggestion. Whenever you are troubled, and feel your peace has fled, you must speak to your angel guardian. Ask your little heavenly soldier to hasten to your assistance and obtain the graces you need to recover your peace. This is the perfect request from you because there is nothing heaven likes better than to help a soul in the world be at peace. You see, we know how important it is and you might say that these graces are easily obtained when the request comes from you. So say this when you are losing your spiritual balance and your peace, "Dearest angel guardian, I desire to serve Jesus by remaining at peace. Please obtain for me the graces necessary to maintain His divine peace in my heart." You will not be disappointed, little ones. The graces will come to you.

Points To Ponder:

- *Children, your Jesus has asked that you walk in peace. He needs this from you, as His plan cannot be realized unless you cooperate with that request.*

- *Whenever you are troubled, and feel your peace has fled, you must speak to your angel guardian. Ask your little heavenly soldier to hasten to your assistance and the graces you need to recover your peace.*

- *So say this when you are losing your spiritual balance and peace, "Dearest angel guardian, I desire to serve Jesus by remaining at peace. Please obtain for me the graces necessary to maintain His divine peace in my heart."*

- *You will not be disappointed, little ones. The graces will come to you.*

September 8, 2004

Blessed Mother

My children, how often I have looked upon you, surrounded by God's angels but feeling so alone. These angels have soft little hearts and they grieve with you when you are sad. So often they seek to comfort you with heavenly thoughts but you do not accept these ideas. Allow these beautiful thoughts into your hearts and you will feel the consolation with which the angels seek to bless you. Again I say, and I understand that I am repeating myself, you must spend time in silence so that we can place these lovely thoughts in your hearts. You understand that communicating with heaven is not like communicating with earth. We do not shout, usually, and you must listen with your soul. In days past, there was not this constant noise. Children, think about why the enemy never leaves you in peace. It is like a child's attempt to distract someone so that bad news cannot be communicated about him. When you feel distracted, and feel your peace is slipping from you, ask yourself how much time during that particular day you spent in silence, contemplating God. I am certain that it was not enough. So find silence. Seek it out. Value it. Understand that this is not wasted time, but the most important time of your day.

Points To Ponder:

- *These angels have soft little hearts and they grieve when you are sad. So often they seek to comfort you with heavenly thoughts but you do not accept these ideas.*

- *Allow these beautiful thoughts into your hearts and you will feel the consolation with which the angels seek to console you.*

- *Again I say, and I understand that I am repeating myself, you must spend time in silence so that we can place these lovely thoughts in your hearts.*

- *When you feel distracted, and feel your peace is slipping from you, ask yourself how much time during that particular day you spent in silence, contemplating God.*

- *So find silence. Seek it out. Value it. Understand that this is the most important time of your day.*

September 9, 2004

Blessed Mother

Little children of the Kingdom, you must be joyful. Rest in the idea that you belong to the family of God. This fact will not change. God will never reject you. You have no worries in that regard. Your mistakes, your sins, your failings, none of these things will cause you to lose your eternity with God as long as you repent and try to follow Jesus. Dear child of my Immaculate Heart, sit still for a moment and think about the family of God. We are a very big, very strong family indeed. There is none stronger, none bigger. Your Father is all-powerful. His angels have every bit of wisdom at their disposal. You have constant access to this. Once you understand that the wisdom required to serve need not come from you, you will feel lighter. Be joyful, please. Your eternity is safe so there is nothing else to concern you. If you think this way, you will serve in freedom and you will serve with ease. I, Mary, wish this for you. Your service need not be a time of pain, despite the necessary sacrifices. But remember, when you are sacrificing worldly things, that you will be giving these things up anyway. It is wrong to be too attached to things that do not last. The inevitable relinquishing of these things is what causes you pain. Ask the angels to help you with this and everything. God has given the angels assignments so they know what He wills. Meditate often on the beautiful thought that your constant companions know God's will for you.

Points To Ponder:

- *Little children of the kingdom, you must be joyful. Rest in the idea that you belong to the family of God.*

- *Your mistakes, your sins, your failings, none of these will cause you to lose your eternity with God as long as you repent and try to follow Jesus.*

- *Dear children of my Immaculate Heart, sit still for a moment and think about the family of God.*

- *Once you understand that the wisdom required to serve need not come from you, you will feel lighter.*

- *Be joyful, please. Your eternity is safe so there is nothing else to concern you.*

- *God has given the angels assignments that they know what He wills. Meditate often on the beautiful thought that your constant companions know God's will for you.*

September 10, 2004

Blessed Mother

There are many types of angels, all with different missions, in the heavenly Kingdom. The angels that work on earth are very special and have the greatest of love for humanity. Children, you have not experienced heavenly love in the purest sense and will not until the time of your earthly death. Until that time, you must believe us when we tell you that you are loved most perfectly. One such example of the love that is boundless in heaven is the love of your angel guardian for you. Your angel guardian knows you better than any human being could possibly know you because your angel guardian has known you for eternity. Before you were created, in the physical sense, you were known by this being of light. This creation of God is filled with His love and His love flows through His angels to you. When we talk to you about the beginning of Christ's return, part of what we are discussing is the flow of Christ's love through each one of you. So be filled with joy that this little angel of God accompanies you everywhere. God's love flows through this angel into your soul. If you are welcoming of this love, then it can flow through you and into other souls also. How beautiful this process is and how it binds God's family together. When everyone in the heavenly family is together, there will be a seamless flow of love. We will know nothing but peace and happiness then, children, and you will understand what it is I have tried to tell you. Be at peace, little ones. Your mother is with you.

Points To Ponder:

- *There are many types of angels, all with different missions in the heavenly kingdom. The angels that work on earth are very special and have the greatest love for humanity.*

- *One such example of the love that is boundless in heaven is the love of your guardian angel for you.*

- *Your angel guardian knows you better than any human being could possibly know you because your angel guardian has known you for eternity.*

- *When we talk to you about the beginning of Christ's return, part of what we are discussing is the flow of Christ's love through each one of you. So be filled with joy that this little angel of God's accompanies you everywhere. God's love flows through this angel into your soul.*

- *How beautiful this process is and how it binds God's family together.*

- *Be at peace, little ones. Your Mother is with you.*

September 11, 2004

Blessed Mother

Little children, how I love you. A mother's love is so forgiving and understanding because a mother knows her children well. I am that way with you. I know you each so well and understand your little struggles and troubles. Our God, in His goodness and mercy, has given me the greatest of honor here in heaven. I have complete discretion on how to instruct the angels to intervene on earth. I walk only in the Divine Will, you see, as do we all here, so there is no reason for conflict. You must ask me for help and I will send angels to assist you and to assist those around you. As I watch you, I sometimes feel my heart aching for you because you feel alone. When you come here you will see that you were never alone for a moment. You will not be left alone. Consider Jesus and His total love for you. Would He abandon you? Of course not. He sees your pain and sends little angels and earthly souls to help you. Sometimes you are not ready to be helped so you do not accept the help He has sent. He understands and waits, watching for another opportunity when perhaps you will be more open to Him. You are cherished. Be joyful, little ones. Your mother loves you and will never leave you. I send angels to you on each and every day, after considering what tasks you have undertaken for the Kingdom. There is nothing left to chance, particularly with heaven's work. Cast away fear, little children of God's family. You have no reason to be afraid. Our promises will not be forgotten, as often happens with earthly promises. You can rely on these words from heaven and you can rely on Us.

Points To Ponder:

- *Little children, how I love you. A mother's love is so forgiving and understanding because a mother knows her children well. I am that way with you.*

- *Our God, in His goodness and mercy, has given me the greatest of honor here in heaven. I have complete discretion on how to instruct the angels to intervene on earth.*

- *You must ask me for help and I will send angels to assist you and to assist those around you.*

- *Consider Jesus and His total love for you. Would He abandon you? Of course not. He sees your pain and sends little angels and earthly souls to help you.*

- *Be joyful, little ones. Your Mother loves you and will never leave you. I send angels to you on each and every day, after considering what tasks you have undertaken for the kingdom.*

- *You have no reason to be afraid. Our promises will not be forgotten, as often happens with earthly promises. You can rely on these words from heaven and you can rely on Us.*

Appendix I

Consecration to Your Guardian Angel

Just as the Catholic Church has approved a personal con-secration to Mary, Mother of God (particularly according to the format of St. Louis Marie Grignion de Monfort), and a personal consecration to St. Joseph, Patron of the Universal Church, the Church has also approved a personal consecra-tion by the Christian faithful to their Guardian Angels.

When the individual Christian consecrates himself or her-self to Our Lady, St. Joseph, or one's Guardian Angel, they are not placing the creature in place of the Creator, but on the contrary seeking the fullest powerful intercession by the creature for unity and fidelity to the Creator.

As is the case with Marian Consecration, when we give ourselves to Mary as a gift, she, as Mediatrix of all graces has the spiritual capacity to unite us to Jesus in ways we simply cannot do on our own. The same goal of intimate union with God and a more full obedience to his Divine Will is the goal of consecration to one's Guardian Angel.

One way that you can "free" your Guardian Angel to most fully intercede on your behalf is by making of an act of "consecration" or "gift of yourself" to your Guardian Angel. This allows your Guardian Angel to fully intervene on your behalf since your Angel now has your full consent to receive his greatest possible intercession and protection. God will not force grace upon us. He always respects his most precious gift to each of us, the gift of free will. God will not even force upon us the full protection of the Angel he has given us. God awaits "fiat," our "yes."

A consecration, therefore, is a manifestation of our free and full consent to allow our Angel maximum interceding power to guide us in the ways of Christian holiness and peace. The *"Opus Angelorum Sanctorum"* or "Work of the Holy Angels" is a spiritual movement within the Catholic Church that encourages authentic devotion and consecration to our Guardian Angels.[47]

On May 31, 2000, the Vatican's Congregation for the Doctrine of Faith gave official approval to the following beautiful prayer of Consecration that the Christian faithful can make to their own Guardian Angel[48]:

O Holy Angels of God, here, in the presence of the Triune God, and in the love of Jesus Christ, my Lord and Redeemer, I, (name) a poor sinner, want to make a covenant with you, who are his servants, so that in union with you, I might work with humility and fortitude for the glory of God and the coming of his Kingdom. Therefore, I implore you to assist me, especially in the adoration of God and of the Most Holy Sacrament of the Altar, in the contemplation of the Word and the salvific works of God – in the imitation of Christ and in love of his

Cross in a spirit of expiationin the faithful fulfillment of my mission within the Church, serving humbly after the example of Mary, your Queen. And you, my good guardian angel, who continually behold the face of our Father in heaven, God entrusted me to you in the very beginning of my life. I thank you with all my heart for your loving care. I commit myself to you and promise you my love and fidelity. I beg you: protect me against my own weakness and against the attacks of the wicked spirits; enlighten my mind and my heart so that I may always know and accomplish the will of God, and lead me to union with God the Father, the Son, and the Holy Spirit. Amen.

Appendix II

Chaplet of St. Michael the Archangel

The history of this Chaplet goes back to a devout Servant of God, Antonia d'Astonac, who had a vision of St. Michael. He told Antonia to honor him by nine salutations to the nine Choirs of Angels. St. Michael promised that whoever would practice this devotion in his honor would have, when approaching Holy Communion, an escort of nine angels chosen from each of the nine Choirs. In addition, for those who would recite the Chaplet daily, he promised his continual assistance and that of all the holy angels during life.

The Chaplet of St. Michael

O God, come to my assistance. O Lord, make haste to help me. Glory be to the Father, etc.

[Say one Our Father and three Hail Marys after each of the following nine salutations in honor of the nine Choirs of Angels]

1. By the intercession of St. Michael and the celestial

Choir of Seraphim may the Lord make us worthy to burn with the fire of perfect charity. Amen.

2. By the intercession of St. Michael and the celestial Choir of Cherubim may the Lord grant us the grace to leave the ways of sin and run in the paths of Christian perfection. Amen.

3. By the intercession of St. Michael and the celestial Choir of Thrones may the Lord infuse into our hearts a true and sincere spirit of humility. Amen.

4. By the intercession of St. Michael and the celestial Choir of Dominations may the Lord give us grace to govern our senses and overcome any unruly passions. Amen.

5. By the intercession of St. Michael and the celestial Choir of Virtues may the Lord preserve us from evil and falling into temptation. Amen.

6. By the intercession of St. Michael and the celestial Choir of Powers may the Lord protect our souls against the snares and temptations of the devil. Amen.

7. By the intercession of St. Michael and the celestial Choir of Principalities may God fill our souls with a true spirit of obedience. Amen.

8. By the intercession of St. Michael and the celestial Choir of Archangels may the Lord give us perseverance in faith and in all good works in order that we may attain the glory of Heaven. Amen.

9. By the intercession of St. Michael and the celestial Choir of Angels may the Lord grant us to be protected by them in this mortal life and conducted in the life to come in Heaven. Amen.

Say one Our Father in honor of each of the following leading Angels: St. Michael, St. Gabriel, St. Raphael and our Guardian Angel.

Concluding prayers:

O glorious prince St. Michael, chief and commander of the heavenly hosts, guardian of souls, vanquisher of rebel spirits, servant in the house of the Divine King and our admirable conductor, you who shine with excellence and superhuman virtue deliver us from all evil, who turn to you with confidence and enable us by your gracious protection to serve God more and more faithfully every day.

Pray for us, O glorious St. Michael, Prince of the Church of Jesus Christ, that we may be made worthy of His promises.

Almighty and Everlasting God, Who, by a prodigy of goodness and a merciful desire for the salvation of all men, has appointed the most glorious Archangel St. Michael Prince of Your Church, make us worthy, we ask You, to be delivered from all our enemies, that none of them may harass us at the hour of death, but that we may be conducted by him into Your Presence. This we ask through the merits of Jesus Christ Our Lord.

Amen.